A STEP INTO MY HEART

JOSEPH R. ADOMAVICIA

Dawn, thank you for your support!
Enjoy!
Joseph R Adomavicia

RP PUBLISHING

A STEP INTO MY HEART

WRITTEN AND ARRANGED BY JOSEPH R. ADOMAVICIA

A Sign of What Is to Come

You call for creativity
I crave the creativity
I enjoy the simplicity,
Implicitly.

CONTENTS

A Poet is a Poem Unwritten	11
A Step into My Heart	13
Even-Keeled	15
Dreaming the Dream Poetic	17
The Poetry in Life	18
Poison Arrow	20
Forsaken	21
And Here I Sit, the Life of the Party	22
On This Day, Deep, Somber and Gray	23
It's Okay to Be Afraid	24
You Can't Hold Me Back	25
Home Psychology	26
Suited in Traits and Actions	28
Fearing Wisely	29
For, I Too, Have Written Darkly	30
Cerulean Wings	32
Ice House Road	33
You and I Must Be	34
On Average, America	35
Light in the Darkness	39
Woman of My Dreams	40
Held Within the Sun	41
You Asked and I Answered	43
On the Wayside	44
Blood Sweat and Tears	45
A Cause Unknown	46
On Watch	47
Serenity	49
My Addiction	50
Love's Equation	51
Of All You Could Have Asked	52
Untangled, Unraveled	53

Sinner's Exile 55
Earn a Dollar to Spend a Dollar 57
The Wires of Life 59
A Walk in the Park (Shakespearean Sonnet) 61
Beyond the Pale 62
Unconnected Connection 63
Love's Duality 64
In This Life or Another 65
Easy-Going Woman 66
Ray of Hope 67
Prominence 68
Sun Rays 69
My Dear Friend 70
Stay on Top of Your Game (An Ode to Edward Segal Inc.) 71
In the Name of Love and Metaphor 73
We Americans Refacing the Nation 74
Pick Some Flowers 76
Till the End of Time 78
Glimpses 79
Something Clever, but Nothing Cliché 81
Straight from the Heart 82
Without You 83
The Rustle of the Leaves 84
Love's Taste 85
If There Is Ever 86
Love's Path 87
All That Is true, Lies in You 88
Cleansing 89
Cup of Joe 90
Without a Worry in the World 91
This One Goes out To... 92

A
STEP INTO MY HEART

JOSEPH R. ADOMAVICIA

A POET IS A POEM UNWRITTEN

A poet is a poem unwritten.

For me,
Joe Adomavicia,
a tools precision
is manufactured
in CNC machinery,
written in a language of codes;
G's, M's, even Cartesian's X's, Y's and Z's,
complete my metal cutting novelties.

A poet is a poem unwritten.

For me,
Joe Adomavicia,
a poem's strength and its frailty
are intrinsic to the writer.
They are the arteries
pumping poetic blood,
dispersing diversity,
evocative attractions
relinquishing darkness
in the soul of the poet.

A poet is a poem unwritten.

For me,
Joe Adomavicia,
there is a destination –
a journey traveled dreaming,
guided by education,
merit and determination.
There is a poet and his poems,
and poems that are the poet,
and in the latter is where I lay –

within my poems
I have found home.

A STEP INTO MY HEART

Take a step into my heart,
talk this talk with me
walk this walk with me,
across creaking boards
and ravaged threads
weathered, battered
and bogged down.

Take a step into my heart,
talk this talk with me
walk this walk with me,
across a wide mouthed river
rapid waters streaming,
moderate overcast,
hunter green pine trees,
line dried dirt paths
leading to a stone castle
without a master key,
but, be forewarned,
a crenellation's arrow loops
compliment a pair of
eagle eyes atop his nest.

Take a step into my heart,
talk this talk with me
walk this walk with me,
travel dimly lit winding halls
to find an open towering set
of ebony chamber doors
jeweled in opal,
follow the scarlet carpet
into center chamber,
set your eyes upon these
walls and decipher,

take a step into my heart
and see what it takes
to be me.

EVEN-KEELED

Even-keeled,
with Uncle Whitman's wit,
begins the voyage
of due time,
and time passing.

I am the
captain of one,
and the
captain of none.

Set to seas untraveled –
my glory has yet to be revealed.

Even-keeled,
with Uncle Whitman's wit,
continues the voyage
of due time,
and time passing.

I am the
captain of one,
and the
captain of none.

Upon my return,
rays of light to illuminate
the shine of integrity acquired.
Let prophets speak
of a man meek,
yet standing tall.

For I am even-keeled –

Captain of one,
and
captain of none.

DREAMING THE DREAM POETIC

Would it be wrong?
Would it be abstract?
If only now I have realized
that me,
after all this time
an ordinary Joe,
is actually worth more than an old,
tails up, rustic, ravished penny?

Would it be wrong?
Would it be abstract?
To say that I think I am,
that me,
an ordinary Joe, is
beginning to see
the poetry in Life?

Would it be wrong?
Would it be abstract?
To say that I think I am,
that me,
an ordinary Joe,
is poetry's poet
and did not even know it?

Would it be wrong?
Would it be abstract?
To say,
that I am,
that me,
an ordinary Joe is
dreaming the dream poetic?

THE POETRY IN LIFE

Take two steps into the outdoors.
Fix your eyes upon the scenery.
Poetry is in everything you hear,
see, taste and touch.

No matter the season,
without much reason,
life is life,
explicit is its beauty.

Can you hear it?
A ravishing red cardinal,
sitting upon his branch
singing songs of hope for a
love to burn on passionately.

Can you see it?
Laying in the grass
on a warm spring afternoon,
white clouds contrasting
the blissful blue sky.

Can you taste it?
Summer is on the brink of emergence,
bringing the best of times.
Family gatherings with foods galore,
along with hot summer days baring
shimmering sunrays that give way to rainy days.

Can you smell it?
A thunderstorm is rolling in and rain is falling
drop by drop, pair by pair,
allowing us to run around in the rain,
enjoying life in all of its elements.

Who knows, maybe you may find your first kiss
within the downpour of a summer day,
willingly dismissing everyday anxiety,
letting in a little bliss
that is the poetry in life.

POISON ARROW

You
landed a
piercing
blow
upon
my
chest;

Spl   it   ti   ng
m   y
fra   gile
he   art
i   n

two,
spilling
love's blood
unto the floor.
Unrelenting pain coursing through,
bringing me to my knees
as the essence of my
mind, soul, and body
is drained from the inside out.

It is hard now –
It is hard all of the time
to breathe and
I am trying my best
to repair the wounds of old,
working my hands
to the point of breaking,
trying to pull this
poison arrow from my chest.

FORSAKEN

Poetry defining the existence
of a being so fragile.
Feelings of entrapment,
the caged bird that does not sing.
Physically and mentally drained,
pained to the point of solitude.
Miserable life trapped in disdain.
Where is the escape from this misery?
Join in the escape, follow toward the light,
running and running to the end of the tunnel.
It is in sight, yet it moves as I move and
further away with every step that is taken
trapped in this hell.

Why is it that I am forsaken?

AND HERE I SIT, THE LIFE OF THE PARTY

And here I sit,
the life of the party –
alone,
desolate,
barren,
music blaring,
people dancing,
lips locking passionately,
and the smell of cigarette smoke
lingering through the air.
And here I sit,
the life of the party –
wondering what, exactly, is wrong with me.
I just cannot see what others see,
it must not be in me genetically,
or I must just be a face in the crowd
waiting to be heard aloud.
Somehow – my voice is too soft you see,
my frame too frail,
demeanor too shy,
and I am simply not
what any of you expect of me.
I can try and dress the part
but I cannot walk the walk,
it is too tough for me mentally
to succumb to your catastrophe.
I wait – and then I wait some more,
I try – and then I try some more.
I pick myself up again
only to be knocked back down.

ON THIS DAY, DEEP, SOMBER AND GRAY

On this day, deep, somber and gray,
rain drops fall all around me,
trickling down from my brow,
all the way down to my chin,
dropping off to the ground,
leaving my skin saturated,
cooling me within.

On this day, deep, somber, and gray,
rain drops fall all around me,
forming puddles on the concrete
to run through, splashing,
celebrating, treasuring
a liberating moment,
finding light in the
dimmest of days.

On this day, deep, somber, and gray
rain drops have fallen all around me,
and now tranquil sun rays have begun
to shine upon me, bursting through
the clouds, warming my body,
replenishing my being,
returning me to my senses,
guiding me to a destination paved in beauty,
following a rainbow to find my pot of gold.

IT'S OKAY TO BE AFRAID

It is okay to be afraid,
there is an indomitable will
inside of you.
And whatever must be shall be,
and this you shall see, but,
do not let yesterday's fears
dissipate the outcome
of tomorrow's possibilities.

It is okay to be afraid,
if a day should come
that would ruffle the feathers of some,
just know you are you
and you is not them –
adjust and readjust if you must, but,
do not let yesterday's fears
dissipate the outcome
of tomorrow's possibilities.

I shall say it once more
before I am done –

It is okay to be afraid,

I swear –
I am too –
you are not alone.

YOU CAN'T HOLD ME BACK

Hit me,
take shots at me,
aim for my face,
take out my arms,
take out my legs,
insult me,
hit me where it hurts,
satisfy your thirst,
I know damn well,
you can't hold me back.

Rip my heart from my chest;
bleed it dry to satisfy
your innermost desires.
The chances of you deterring me from
my goals, my dreams,
what I aspire to be?
Well let's just say,
that you have a better chance
of seeing me quitting all together,
ha, as if that would ever happen.
I know damn well,
You can't hold me back.

So go ahead,
take shots at me,
aim for my face,
take out my arms,
take out my legs,
insult me,
hit me where it **hurts**,
satisfy your thirst,
I know damn well,
you can't hold me back.

HOME PSYCHOLOGY

When I am feeling lonely,
I say to myself;

"Joe, you are not alone.
Look at the family you have;
a mother and father,
three brothers,
nieces and nephews,
uncles and aunts,
cousins and close friends;
and all of us manufacturing
our way to success.

Who can stop us from getting
to the top of the mountain?

Remember,
the only one that can stop us is ourselves.

So is there a reason to feel alone?
I think not."

And within the times
I am engulfed by fear,
I say to myself;

"Joe, you have nothing to fear,
the poetry gear
within your noggin
keeps on loggin'.
Put it on paper,
never falter,
and turn that frown
upside down.

You are going to have those days
where it seems everything is in the way,
but the will to keep on climbing to the top
will instill true timing and your poetry will pop.
Remember,
the only one that can stop you is you.
So is there a reason to be engulfed in fear?
I think not."
But at the end of the day
I chuckle and say to myself,
"What do I know,
I just wrote a poem
about how I talk to myself."

SUITED IN TRAITS AND ACTIONS

I could never figure out what traits
suited a person worse –
a face with happy eyes
complimented by a frown,
or a face with a smile
complimented by sad eyes.

I could never figure out what traits
suited a person worse –
a towering stature with a slouch,
or a towering stature
weighed down by arrogance.

I could never figure out what actions
suited a person worse –
one who barks yet never acts,
or one who acts
but never atones for their actions.

I could never figure out what actions
suited a person worse –
one who preaches love
but does not act upon it,
or one who acts in the name of love
with intention aimed to deceive.

FEARING WISELY

I fear not the death of me,
the death of passion is what I fear.
For, it would be more painful to live –
impossible to love,
walking this earth
without it.

FOR I, TOO, HAVE WRITTEN DARKLY

Write on,
fellow scribe.
Write on.
We are one
you and I,
for I, too,
have written darkly.

Inscribing feelings
blood soaked
onto paper,
saturated with emotion.
Each word,
each line,
stories told of a time
of two hearts
once intertwined.

Write on,
fellow scribe.
Write on.
We are one
you and I,
for I, too,
have felt darkly.

If the road walked
reveals trials unmatched,
stand your ground –
and may my words be
the reason you turn back.

For, I too,
have felt alone.

Reacquire purpose,
sustain life,
shake the shackles
of despondent depression
that left you withered, battered
and broken down.

Write on,
fellow scribe.
Write on.
We are one
you and I,
for, I too,
have risen from
the depths of darkness.

CERULEAN WINGS

Even in the cold
Beauty stands bold
With Leafless trees
And Hints of snow
Covering the limbs
And Maybe
Some day soon
Blue jays
Will come and
Sing a song,
Maybe two,
With their
Delightful
Cerulean wings
Blessing thy ears
With songs of
Serenity
Glazing thy heart
Purifying,
Cleansing,
From within.

ICE HOUSE ROAD

There is a long, beaten, frosted road
with snow capped pine trees lining the streets.
With bright yellows and deep blues
contrasting in the skies overhead.
A starlit sky with a magnificent full moon
as if Vincent van Gogh painted the skies
right before my own two eyes.
Such luxuries in the scenery
make the Ice House even more inviting.
Further down this long, winding road
sits a house with jagged spikes of ice
hanging above the entry ways
of the old, weather-bitten Victorian home,
as if their sole intention was to
protect what was embodied inside.

Such a beauteous scene, but
what is there to protect when
the inside is as hollow as the one who
treads upon its doorsteps?

Where is the meaning in sheltering
an empty house, an empty soul,
when it may be just as easy to knock it down,
or end it all and simply move on?

The truth is that moving on
is never as simple as it proclaims
itself to truly be;
a white lie.
White as the snow that caps the trees
on Ice House Road.

YOU AND I MUST BE

You and I must be
the ocean and sea breeze,
the softness of the sand,
or the gentle ebb and flow
of an early morning tide.

You and I must be
the petals of a luscious red rose,
the intimacy of spring's blossom,
or gentle wind against blades of grass
of vast hills, azure bliss overhead.

You and I must be
the autumnal leaves of great oak trees,
the falling colors dancing in the air,
or a cherry blossom's pink wave
of precious and precarious relation.

You and I must be
the novas within ebony skies,
the vibrancy of Saturn's rings,
or the gravitational pull
of every atom within our existence,
keeping each other's love in orbit.

ON AVERAGE, AMERICA

On average,
statistics show
students that do their
homework regularly
receive better grades
on their tests,
maybe even
live better lives.

If this is the case,
why is it that the
appointed and reappointed
leaders of America, disappoint?

No excuse for the average Joe,
if we don't take the time
to do our own homework,
govern collectively our lives,
work together
as we preach
to our children?

Wake up America.

My mistake.

Apologize.

Pardon me, begging,
words too brash,
wouldn't want to hurt
anyone's feelings now,
or would I?

On average,
statistics show
children that are regularly bullied,
their soul's stripped bare –
these children, our children,
ashamed, fearful,
so much–
they have grown unafraid
to take
their own lives.
Laws passed, hotlines provided.
Nonetheless, everyday
the innocent harassed,
the outcomes a known forecast.
Are we not responsible
for each and every event?
Wake up America.
My mistake.
Apologize.
School shootings
almost weekly,
a news event that now lasts,
maybe, twenty-four hours.
Do we need them to occur
daily
before we make it that they
never happen,
not once, only never?
Wake up America.
My mistake.

Apologize.

Brutish honesty,
who's got time for that
when you can just
change the channel,
go on to the next poem?

My intent
clear.

Get apoplectic!

Intended to strike,
the "it's ok" feelings of the
cowards who sit back,
including us,
who let these insanities
occur and reoccur.

Is that not the definition of crazy?

On average,
based on my observation,
the land of the free has been
reorganized by those
caring for themselves,
lining their pockets with
the lazy approval,
we silent Americans
silently
permit, elect.

Let us give thanks this week,
our lives, so far untouched,
but does not our acceptance
of all these deaths held so cheap
dishonor our freedom,
bile our palate,
make us choke on the turkey?

Has our notion of freedom
become so self-centered,
diminished, tarnished,
even
corrupted?

America, on average,
we cannot be
who we want to be,
a "United State",
if we are content
to be
on average.

LIGHT IN THE DARKNESS

I fear, that sometimes in life
we all go through things
that will push us to the brink
but, know that amongst these
bitter feelings within our hearts
there is a will to push on and be
better than one could imagine.
Stay strong my fellow scribe
for better times are to come
and one can only feel distraught
to the point of rock bottom
and if that point in your life occurs
you must remember that there is
light in darkness and you will
prevail through any hardship.

WOMAN OF MY DREAMS

My aim is not to find
the woman of my dreams,
but it is to find she who
urges me to dream,
and dreams alongside me.

My aim is not to find
the woman of my dreams,
but it is to find she who
can silence my screams
when nightmares
take hold of my dreams.

My aim is not to find
the woman of my dreams,
but it is to find she who
is both the compliment
and supplement
to my geometry.

My aim is not to find
the woman of my dreams,
but it is to find she who
sees me as I see her,
nothing more nothing less,
two hearts concur,
beating as one
bar none.

HELD WITHIN THE SUN

Just in case you are wondering
if I am like all those other men,
my dear you are mistaken,
my love is yours for the taking.

I will not tell you
what you want to hear
but what you need to hear,
and in the face of adversity
whether it be sweet or sour,
I will speak of truths without fear.

Just in case you are wondering
if I am like all those other men,
my dear you are mistaken,
my love is yours for the taking.

I would rather
let my actions speak
to you in ways my words
cannot, holding meaning,
far beyond the glittered horizon
in which, it be, held within the sun.

Just in case you are wondering
if I am like all those other men,
my dear you are mistaken,
my love is yours for the taking.

I will not tell you
what you want to hear
but what you need to hear,
saying the sky is blue year round
when we know even the bluest sky
bares a hint of grey, but, to take your

hand, withstanding the worst of the storm
would be proof enough to reassure you.
Just in case you are wondering
if I am like all those other men,
my dear you are mistaken,
my love is yours for the taking.

YOU ASKED AND I ANSWERED

When you asked me
if I would write for you,
I laughed, and answered,
"I don't even write for myself,
I don't write at all really,
I am just a vessel.
Poetry writes me
and flows through me,
endlessly,
for all of the world to see."

ON THE WAYSIDE

In witnessing a small,
cerulean-winged, white-breasted blue jay
inch itself to the edge of the highest tree branch,
on a day, grass blanketed in snow, a medallion of gold
illuminating a clear, azure sky,
creating a harmonic stage of glory
for it to sing songs courageously,
proving dreams are attainable,
when you leave fear
on the wayside.
Leave the past behind,
cast it out of mind.
Relish what you see
for it soon will shape
who you aim to be.

In witnessing a second small,
onyx winged, red-orange breasted robin
inch itself to the edge of a wilted tree branch,
swooping down, taking flight, fluttering its elegant wings,
teaching a lesson, reminding even
the most frightening trials of life,
are that of a small nuisance
when you leave fear
on the wayside.
Leave the past behind,
cast it out of mind.
Relish what you see
for it soon will shape
who you aim to be.

BLOOD, SWEAT, AND TEARS

My brothers
stand tall beside me,
through blood, sweat, and tears.
Like when Gram and Uncle Bob passed,
no doubt, the river was high those days,
but, we bolstered each other's spirits,
learning to reminisce on the times we shared
with Gram cooking her "secret recipe" meatballs,
or cheering on Silver Charm with Uncle Bob
to take home the triple crown.

My brothers
stand tall beside me,
through blood, sweat, and tears.
As mentors, inspiring
guiding rays of vigilance,
grinding it out, milling and turning
our way through scorching summer days
and frigid winter storms.
Manufacturing our way
to the plateau of success,
thousandth by thousandth,
shaping, honing, sharpening,
each others wits through,

B
s l
r o
a o
e d
T S
d w
n e
A a
t

A CAUSE UNKNOWN

Life moves on, or at least
that's what I tell myself, but,
I do wonder why women
like my poetry but not me,
for, my words are me,
are they not?

Life moves on, or at least,
that's what I tell myself, but,
I do wonder why men
call themselves friends,
when in the end,
they play pretend.

Life moves on, or at least,
that's what I tell myself, but,
I do wonder why
the good die young,
forced to leave behind
sonorous songs unsung.

Life moves on, or at least,
that's what I tell myself, but,
I do wonder why
the blood of innocence
is shed, left splattered,
for a cause unknown.

ON WATCH

Another shooting up the street –
turbid feelings arise,
a thirty six year old shot
while the suspect flees the crime
from a street that interjects mine.
It seems like just last week
I was about ten years old,
out in the backyard playing
wiffle, and kick ball
with my brothers and our friends
as a community.

And now at twenty three
I am on watch
while my niece and nephew run around out back,
play in the pool,
and make mud pies under the tree
my family and I planted,
eleven some odd years ago.

Another shot from up the street –
Is when you hear your neighbor
two houses up yell out
from the second story,
"hey Ma you got that eight ball?"
And again turbid feelings arise
they make me wonder,
were you all raised vacuous,
unmoved by the blaring fact
there is a community around you,
or was it inherited
like a family heirloom?

I cannot say that if I were rich
I could try and help this city –
Because how can I contribute
to those that are not willing
enough to strive to be more than
the slum they are perceived to be?

SERENITY

Gracious green fields,
supple and svelte,
caress every
curve of my frame,
beatific blue skies
overhead for miles.
Free is the mind
of time passing,
of troubles massing,
whimsical white clouds,
willowy winds,
blowing my brown hair
off to the side.
Heart, eyes and mind
awed and anchored
where serenity resides.

Alas,

the setting of the sun
has arrived,
it has begun,
pinks and blues
through and through.
Remarkable reflection,
synonymous symmetry,
what more could one ask for?
Eyes entranced, held captive
until my lids begin to shut,
just as the sun falls below the

H o r i z o N

MY ADDICTION

If I lost my vision at least
I wouldn't be able to see you anymore.
If I lost my hearing at least
I wouldn't be able to hear your lies anymore.
If I lost my sense of scent, touch, and taste,
I'd be free from my addiction;

I'd be free of you.

LOVE'S EQUATION

To you, love is a fraction
with zero in the denominator.
Undefined, vacant, unapparent
and no matter the ideal
you conceive to be real,
this is what your actions
have led me to believe.

To you, love is a fraction
with zero in the numerator.
Zero, zilch, nothing, nada.
And no matter the ideal
you conceive to be real,
this is what your actions
have lead me to believe.

To me, love is an integer with
a zero for an exponent.
Two numbers work together,
in unison baring a solution of One.
And no matter the ideal
I conceive to be real,
this is what my experiences
have lead me to believe.

To me, love is a trigonometric identity.
Two terms whose appearance
shows the opposite, but indeed
are equal to one another.
And no matter the ideal
I conceive to be real,
this is what my experiences
have lead me to believe.

OF ALL YOU COULD HAVE ASKED

Of all you could have asked,
you chose to ask me
to write for you.
And though it disappoints
my sorrow extends your reach,
but, there was never once a time
when I could part
with a piece of my heart
to whom it was not worthy.

UNTANGLED, UNRAVELED

It is all over now.
My heart,
your heart,
untangled,
unraveled.
A kiss farewell
was all I could muster,
to send you on your way.
When I heard the trembling in your voice,
I knew something was amiss
within those hurt soaked, dilated eyes.
The smell of alcohol, and smoke-filled exhales choked me,
along with the fact that you looked like you did when I first met you;
with your eyes that told a story of affliction and self infliction,
the smile you wore that was broken long ago,
long, frizzy, brown hair that showed you did not care,
and your "walls of blue", as you called them,
stood tall once again.
You know I don't hate you,
I only hate the decisions you made,
that shredded my heartstrings into one million pieces.
I could not hate the love and light you gifted my life.
But, unfortunately, this is the way it must be,
no more you and me,
a decision that requires the utmost precision,
cutting ties the love in our heart and eyes created.
To start a new journey without you,
to journal and write my times onto the page,
carrying on without rage filled discontent in my temperament.
And, in these last words to you,
I will tell you one last time that
"I love you."

But,
it is all over now; my heart,
your heart,
untangled,
unraveled.
With a kiss goodbye,
to send you on your way.

SINNER'S EXILE

This Eve before the
night of the holy birth,
time before the pre-morn of
children-bantered pleasured-shouting.
An adult discussion,
a different kind of present
unwrapped,
a Betrayal disclosed,
more bid fare-thee-well.

She proclaims;

"Who gifts such
evil deeds
on Christmas Eve?

You sinner,
your benevolent
gift of Deceit
well-received.

Who you made love in sheets
not Mine,
rid you of my love,
gift her my love?

Your deMeanor;
four freedoms from
sorrow, regret, anguish and hurt,
the new born children in my manger.
Go,
be free
with her,
without me.

Go along with her and
die in the childbirth of
your sinner's delight.
Into the night,
drive,
with filthy, ice-frosted
windows.
Go.
Drive off.

Into sinner's exile.

EARN A DOLLAR TO SPEND A DOLLAR

Earn a dollar
to spend a dollar,
does it even
matter anymore?

Good ol' George
makes the world go 'round.

We all know, or at least
we should by now,
it doesn't matter –
upper class or poor,
what we have sewn
is now theirs to own,
reaping what we condone.

Earn a dollar
to spend a dollar,
does it even
matter anymore?

Good ol' Grant
makes the world go 'round.

A few hundred,
a couple twenties.
What thought to be plenty,
is no more,
but to be sure
here's some more
to settle the score.

Earn a dollar
to spend a dollar,

does it even,
matter anymore?

Good ol' Franklin
makes the world go 'round.

The television speaks,
the internet leaks,
selling the meaning of life
in convoluted progressions,
newly acquired possessions,
seen as necessary to survive.

Earn a dollar
to spend a dollar,
does it even
matter anymore?

Good ol' Benjamin
makes the world go 'round.

THE WIRES OF LIFE

The wires of life have frayed.
And I am not sure
when it started.

Am I the only one
who feels the wires of life
have frayed?

I doubt it,
but a solution
I have pondered;

Revert –
Revert back to a time
when life was not so
juxtaposed.

A time when self absorption
was not the contortion
of the modern mind
and a hint of selflessness
filled you with graciousness.

The wires of life have frayed.

A time when there was not
a question whether
God governed or the
government governed
God.

Am I the only one
who feels the wires of life
have frayed?

I doubt it.
But a solution,
I have pondered;

Revert –

Revert back to a time
when life was not so
juxtaposed.

A time when the average
person's goal was to make
an honest living rather than
milking the system, weaseling
their way into the easiest way out.

The wires of life have frayed.

A time when there was
not a question whether
people should fear
the government or
the government
should fear its people.

Am I the only one
who feels the wires of life
have frayed?

I doubt it,
but at least
I was not afraid
to say it.

A WALK IN THE PARK (SHAKESPEAREAN SONNET)

Autumn's bright blue sky, captured my mind's eye,
vivid maple leaves fall from trembling limbs,
autumn's winds greet, touch, and then kiss goodbye
strolling through the park; humming gentle hymns
staring at the fractured, pale, dried up dirt
paying mind to the great, tall maple tree
soaking the imagery up; keenly alert,
gazing far beyond leaving me with glee
colors of red, orange, and yellow,
happily knowing not everyone has got 'em,
has left me gleaming and oh, so mellow
find your way back to me, dearest Autumn
remind me that, although leaves are leaving,
I will stroll through; left in awe, perceiving.

BEYOND THE PALE

Beyond the pale

my life's on repeat,

listen.

Take a seat at my table, hear told a tale of cracked feet from
walking unmarked trails of cold concrete where ground freezing
battered my being into what once was silent and now whole howls
in small undistinguished anguished pieces of stone screams,
beyond the pale, beyond the pale,
glance upon my face, my mind,
beyond the pale,
beyond the pale.

UNCONNECTED CONNECTION

Although I have not met her yet,
I know she is my birch tree
in a forest of pine cloaked in snow.
Waiting as I am, to sit by her,
underneath the clouds.

Although I have not met her yet,
I know she is a star upon the sky
with autumn in her eyes and
summer's warmth in her touch.

Although I have not met her yet,
I know she is there, in the fields,
smiling, with a daisy in her hair,
complementing her extravagance,
humming songs with cadence
fit soothe my ears.

Although I have not met her yet,
I know we both are an
unconnected connection.
Somehow, someway, eventual,
abstract in my reality,
as destiny is to mystery.

LOVE'S DUALITY

Your love is like artificial sweetener;
sweet to the tongue, bitter to my insides,
and keeps me coming back for more.

Your love is like Cobain's cocaine;
intricate, rapturous, serpentine,
and keeps me coming back for more.

Your love is like Marilyn's heroin;
chasing the dragon leaves me dragging
and keeps me coming back for more.

Your love is like Marley's Mary Jane;
mind in a fog, immersed in the clouds,
and keeps me coming back for more.

Your love is like Jimi's yellow sunshine;
a rush, a euphoric sensation, a hallucination
and keeps me coming back for more.

IN THIS LIFE OR ANOTHER

If we see each other again,
whether it be in this life or another,
I pray we see each other and you don't walk by,
because, I will be there waiting to see your face.

If we see each other again,
whether it be in this life or another,
I pray we choose not to hold our tongues,
because, I will be there listening for your voice.

If we see each other again,
whether it be in this life or another,
I pray you make effort to climb any mountain for me,
because, I will be there at the top, awaiting your grace.

If we see each other again,
whether it be in this life or another,
I pray you have sought meaning greater than I,
because, I will be there, praying to hear of your success.

EASY-GOING WOMAN

I need an easy-going woman
to rock my world and send me into a swirl –
the type of woman
with the dialect of an intellect –
she who speaks with indubitable rhetoric.

I need an easy-going woman
to rock my world and send me into a swirl –
the type of woman
who can decipher my mind's hieroglyph –
she who could prove the amiss a myth.

Easy-going woman
how I need you,
oh, yes I do –

Find your way to me
and we could run true,
filling the lines of our worlds.

Easy-going woman
how I need you,
oh, yes I do –

I need an easy-going woman
to rock my world and send me into a swirl –
the type of woman
who wants an easy-going man –
he who translates dreams into reality.

RAY OF HOPE

A ray of hope
found its way through my blinds
and has shone onto the
cold hardwood floor beneath my feet
and I thought,
what a day to be me.
Every moment up to this second
I have survived –
understanding
the sun sets,
the sun rises,
and I am me
undoubtedly.

PROMINENCE

If there was one thing I knew
to be true about you,
it would be the sun rises
within the iris of your eyes.
And when your gaze meets mine
I see the truest –
the divine.

If there was one thing I knew
to be true about you,
it would be the fact your touch
is able to mend the oceanic rift of reclusion
tarnishing my consciousness.

If there was one thing I knew
to be true about you,
it would be the confidence of your nature,
has will enough to enrapture
the dimness of an impending storm.

If there was one thing I knew
to be true about you,
it would be the sun sets
to the harmony of your existence –
the prominence in my world.

SUN RAYS

Two little bundles of joy –
Dylan, the brutal baby boy,
Ariya, the gracious baby girl –
have led my life in a upwards twirl.

Watching you grow is so surreal.
Such innocence and beauty, it's unreal.
Your Uncle Joe Joe loves you so so much.
An unconditional love, free of any crutch.

Each day brings a new climax,
loving you more and more.
My happiness driven to the max.
Here is to wondrous days galore.

Though there may be days
where a monster may appear,
fret not my glorious sun rays,
we will cast it away without a fear.

MY DEAR FRIEND

Looking down through the cloud,
you are free from blame; if you weren't so proud.
I haven't been the same since that day.
Living through honesty; for it is my way.

Taken from this earth
without a chance to unearth
all the days that could have come.
Now your gone, breaking hearts of some.

How I would love to see you.
On the contrary, how about you?
Selfish; I truly know I am.
Proud; I truly know I am.

Wishing I could regress
to the day before the mess.
To say "I love you and I'll miss you."
My dear friend, Dwight Nadeau.

Death isn't just an obstacle,
and will never be reversible,
only painstakingly rehearsable
and in my life; Proximal.

STAY ON TOP OF YOUR GAME (AN ODE TO EDWARD SEGAL INC.)

I'm tellin' ya',
stay on top of your game.

If not,
the only wall you will land on
is the goddamned wall of shame.
No one ever told ya' to play dead,
stand up on your own two feet.
Never admit defeat,
beat it into your head
till all of that doubt
is good and dead.

I'm tellin' ya',
stay on top of your game.

If not,
you'll never find fame.
You'll see a shameful frame
of your face in disgust
and a whole lotta lust
for the aplomb of those
who knew better to trust
in themselves.

I'm tellin' ya',
stay on top of your game.

If not,
who knows
where the wind might blow
or which way the currents will pull you.

Understand the presentiments of life
are of great value if you look through
crystalline eyes and not the opaque.

IN THE NAME OF LOVE AND METAPHOR

In the name of love and metaphor
I bring a rose not to say I love you,
because unconditionally
I would say it 100 times over again –
but I bring a rose to pluck the petals
and watch them dance
their way to the ground
to reside beside our feet.
And while my hands rest gently upon your cheeks,
I know by pressing my lips against the warmth of yours
I would hear the sounds of our hearts pumping in unison
and I would feel your taste as I inhaled your embrace,
savoring most importantly –
the fact that we as the flower and the petals
of what once was and will be,
is willing to live and die,
fulfilling destiny
in the name of love and metaphor.

WE AMERICANS REFACING THE NATION

Think of our country
as one big puzzle.

Each piece fits snug
into but one or two others,
there is no
great art in that.
Are we but
a small pretense?

Artfully pretending
that we are all
just one poem,
same puzzle.

Those who would
categorize, segregate,
instinctually face-divide.

Can a face fully function when
parted by color, faith,
puzzle pieces, eyes, ears, cut off,
insular, singular, dissected entities,
a solitary piece,
a completed poem be?

It cannot be so.

The different pieces,
individual unique shaped.
Yet, as a babe to old man,
the face the same, yet
ever changing,
the only constancy,
the change of change.

Refacing the nation.

There are pseudo-trigger pullers.

Dividers, our politicians.
Lawyers, who sue for the
profits of division,
not for Justice.
We are the electors
of those who proclaim
bigotry
in our name.

So let us
segregate ourselves,
in Unity,

Let us categorize ourselves,
as
we, Americans,
one nation that never ceases to
reface for the better.

PICK SOME FLOWERS

Pick some flowers
and drop them by my grave.
Read my poems and pass them on –
may your tears form a river
to carry you on your way,
for another day
is not too far away.

Smile as we always have
and remember me not
in the worst of my days,
but when the lost found home
and when our hearts felt glory.
Play as we played,
work as we worked,
side by side,
and in each other we could confide.
And though now it be in spirit,
inherit me.
For we stand as one –
my friends –
my family.

Pick some flowers
and drop them by my grave.
Read my poems and pass them on –
may your tears form a river
to carry you on your way,
for another day
is not too far away.

If my death
meant internal peace
for whom
I have inflicted pain,

would the price be too high
for my beloved?
Or should my suffering
speak of the guarantees
of my eternal emotional freedom
to live eternally –
or shall I be damned for it?

TILL THE END OF TIME

You can try and reach to me
from now till the end of time,
but the truth of the matter is
this fire's blaze burns no longer,
due to shallow waters you ponder.

You can try and reach to me
from now till the end of time,
but the truth of the matter is
a rose's thorn only pierces the
hands of those who grab its stem.

You can try and reach to me
from now till the end of time,
but the truth of the matter is
a lion's roar is at its loudest
when its dignity is at stake.

You can try and reach to me
from now till the end of time,
but the truth of the matter is
a tide can only come so far up shore
before it recedes back into the sea.

You can try and reach to me
from now till the end of time,
but the truth of the matter is
the mere thought of you,
the mere thought of us, must die.

GLIMPSES

I catch myself thinking of you
here and there by the river,
knee deep in crisp currents,
skipping rocks and fishing
for palm-sized sun fish
or the occasional rainbow trout
to take a bite and make our day.

I catch myself thinking of you
here and there riding our bikes,
up and down the hills,
working a sweat going up
and when we soared down
the wind; oh, the wind,
it felt liberating.
We could let go and take off
given the wings.

I catch myself thinking of you
here and there in the backyard,
you as the quarterback,
and I was the tight end.
You would yell "Joe, go deep," and boom,
we connected for a touchdown pass,
and met each other halfway to celebrate.

I catch myself thinking of you
here and there cannon balling
into the pool splashing water,
out of it as if it came free,
and when it was time
for dinner we would be pruned
and red as lobsters, so much,
you would think we were dinner.

I catch myself thinking of you
here and there daydreaming
about memories we shared,
and when every one of them started,
everyone of them ended,
descended,
my dear departed.

SOMETHING CLEVER BUT, NOTHING CLICHÉ.

I have been thinking
of something clever,
but nothing cliché.
A single rose or an orchid
simply would not do,
no, it would never be enough
to compliment your beauty.
But, maybe, if I sang a line,
even two, you would see
beyond my off-pitched voice.
I only sing to fit your tune,
to see you smile brighter
than sunshine on the ocean.
I have been thinking of you
as more than a lover,
but nothing cliché.
To say Romeo and Juliet,
two star struck lovers,
would doom me
right from the start.
But, what if I offered
you my hand to dance
under a star kissed sky,
would you accept my offer?
I dance to match your step,
and would take your hand,
because there is no other
in heart or mind.

STRAIGHT FROM THE HEART

Straight from the heart,
from me to you,
I knew it from the start
that you were my type of woman.
The way we smile and laugh,
the way we talk and crack jokes,
the way we click on several levels.

Straight from the heart,
from me to you,
I knew it from the start
that you were my type of woman.
The way I feel, is so for real,
baby, it's me who wants you,
in the winter, spring, summer and fall.

Straight from the heart,
from me to you,
I knew it from the start
that you were my type of woman,
so, here it goes,
straight from the heart,
I ask, "May I be your man?"

The man who
loses himself in your eyes.
The man who
you can depend on undoubtedly.
The man to
taste the grace that rests on your lips.
The man to
feel passion that only comes
straight from the heart.

WITHOUT YOU

Oh, whatever would I do
if I were to lose you?
Roses in my eyes; love derived
garden of emotion, I'm not surprised.

Oh, whatever would I do
if I were to lose you?
My tears set in motion,
quantities rivaling an ocean.

Oh, whatever would I do
if I were to lose you?
Though death is eventual,
my love for you is perpetual.

Oh, whatever would I do
if I were to lose you?
My mind to be lost in space,
never found again, gone, without a trace.

Oh, whatever would I do
if I were to lose you?
Instinctively and intellectually, I'd live for you,
for it would be the least I could do.

THE RUSTLE OF THE LEAVES

I spoke softly
to the winds of old
as they blew through
the rustle of the leaves.

Where is it you go so soon after
you have swept by my skin,
and if my will leads me to follow you,
would you continue to do so as well?

I spoke softly
to the winds of old
as they blew through
the rustle of the leaves.

The abulia of my essence
has left me a wayward soul,
yet, regardless of your choice
I shall await your return.
For one day,
my wings will spread
and will take the grace,
within the trace
of your guidance.

LOVE'S TASTE

The beauty of getting to know someone,
is accepting them for their flaws, bright spots,
and everything in between, through the unseen.

The beauty of getting to know someone,
is accepting the fact you learn to love again
and leave behind the troubles of the past.

The beauty of getting to know someone,
is accepting the fact that vulnerabilities
and all possibilities are out in the open.

The beauty of getting to know someone,
is cherishing all of the special moments
and relishing love's taste in a new flavor.

The beauty of getting to know someone
is cherishing a simple walk in the park,
and the moment when hands lace for the first time.

The beauty of getting to know someone
is cherishing the fact someone knows you
and will continue to cherish you as you do them.

IF THERE IS EVER

If there is ever a moment,
you don't feel beautiful,
tell me. I'll remind you of
how much I adore every
inch of your existence.

If there is ever a moment,
you feel alone, call my name.
I'll be on my way to fill the void
with smiles, love and laughter,
or even a silent companion;
a shoulder to rest your head upon.

If there is ever a moment,
your heart feels broken,
no need to call the doctor;
I'll be the one to tend
to your wounds,
kiss it, and make it all better.

If there is ever a moment,
your soul feels lost,
please, don't worry;
the best part of being
soul mates is there
will always be a piece of you
inside of me.

LOVE'S PATH

Beyond the constant ringing,
still I listen, for blue birds singing,
and as for my blurred vision,
I understand the sun rises
just as the sun sets;
a sure bet, life moves on.
Beyond my coarse, battered hands,
still I crave, to touch another's life again,
and as for this broken heart,
I understand love's path will rise,
Clotho spins the thread of life,
Lachesis measures its length,
and Atropos the Inevitable,
severs with abhorred shears.

ALL THAT IS TRUE, LIES IN YOU

I'm not sure what it is yet,
and I can't quite put my finger on it,
but, maybe, it is the sparkle in your eye,
or the way you talk to me
as if you have always known me.

I'm not sure what it is yet,
and I can't quite put my finger on it,
but, maybe, it is in the softness of your touch,
or the way you kiss me just underneath my chin
as if you could taste my love for you on my skin.

I'm not sure what it is yet,
and I can't quite put my finger on it,
but, maybe, it is in the serenity of your aura,
or the way you give me reason to smile
as if all you ever wanted was for me to live a life worthwhile.

I'm not sure what it is yet,
and I can't quite put my finger on it,
but, maybe, it is in the way you sing,
or the way you soothe my wounds,
as if all that was ever true, lies in you.

CLEANSING

No longer afraid of
risk and consequence,
I begin to cleanse my life of
the mundane,
the insane,
breaking the vein
that fuels the hate.
Serving a plate
of righteousness
to he or she who stands against me.
No longer afraid of
risk and consequence,
I begin to cleanse my life of
the fakes, the snakes,
hissing, rattling, slithering,
through nooks and crannies,
with fangs drenched in deceit;
waiting for the opportune moment,
to strike tactfully and precisely.
No longer afraid of
risk and consequence,
here I come,
storming the gates of hell,
face to face
with the harbinger of hate,
determined, steadfast, persevering,
in honor of my dignity.

A CUP OF JOE

So, I'm not the Joe you used to know?
I don't know what you want me to do so,
carry on with your life, you know ?

Is it that hard to see
that I'm living free?
Guilt will not drag me down to be
what you ask all ask of me.

Renew and replenish,
You know time will diminish such selfishness –
A priceless portrait of your belligerent betrayal.

Betrayal never to be forgotten,
your vicious omission
my heart you trodden
my life beat to submission.

If you dance with the devil –
In hell you shall revel.
Articulate your sins with a golden bevel
and blasphemy's foundation is laid level.

So, I'm not the Joe
You used to know,
Well good riddance you know ?

Wind at my back, living to grow.

WITHOUT A WORRY IN THE WORLD

I have come to a point in my life,
where the sun shines bright,
brighter than it ever has before.
A place where I smile freely,
without a worry in the world.

I have come to a point in my life,
where the love that permeates
is within the man I have grown into.
A place where I have pride in who I am,
without a worry in the world.

I have come to a point in my life,
where forgiveness trumps grudges,
and those who have done me wrong are in
a place where they rest in my past,
without a worry in the world.

I have come to a point in my life,
where success is the only option,
and my dreams are within my grasp;
a place where I stand on my own two feet,
without a worry in the world.

THIS ONE GOES OUT TO . . .

This one goes out to all the harlots
who led me to the starlets,
the piece of my heart you ran away with,
I have let go fast and left it in the past.

You taught me a barrel of whiskey gains quality within its age,
so I better learn to let the dust settle before I rage.

This one goes out to all of the demons
who tried tearin' down what I am dreamin'.
I am a new man, with a new plan, my life, in my hands.

You taught me my path may stray from its course,
and woven dreams may become untangled,
so I better learn to discern, or in hell I will burn.

This one goes out to the supposed word lords,
who try to tear apart my poetry like a sword
to the flesh of a warrior who has fallen into discord.

You taught me my artistry defines me,
and I have the last say, it is my shield
against the words of a critic ephemeral.

ABOUT THE AUTHOR

Joseph R. Adomavicia at twenty four years old resides in Waterbury, Connecticut. His full time occupation is a licensed CNC (computer numerical control) Machinist at Edward Segal Incorporated. He is currently a student at Naugatuck Valley Community College pursuing an Associate Degree in Mechanical Engineering and also is pursuing an Associate Degree in Liberal Arts and Sciences. Aside from being one of the editors of Naugatuck Valley Community College's Fresh Ink magazine, the past two years his two poems Cerulean Wings and On Average, America were selected for publication. As for his poetry, it is diverse and stylistically intrinsic to the subject matter. As a writer his means are to portray generosity, inspiration and to be inspired by others. Within his words there are several glimpses of various aspects of life varying from love in its many faces, politics, poems of motivation and inspiration to the natural beauty of the world. He writes with the undying purpose to tell his times through his story written evocatively, inspiringly flowing free for the world to see.

Photographer: Aneil Matthew Younis

CPSIA information can be obtained
at www.ICGtesting.com
Printed in the USA
FFHW011452091118
49283422-53516FF

9 780692 778739

BLACKOUT EDITION

A STEP INTO MY HEART

JOSEPH R. ADOMAVICIA

RP PUBLISHING

A STEP INTO MY HEART

WRITTEN AND ARRANGED BY JOSEPH R. ADOMAVICIA

A Sign of What Is to Come

You call for creativity
I crave the creativity
I enjoy the simplicity,
Implicitly.

CONTENTS

A Poet is a Poem Unwritten 11
A Step into My Heart 13
Even-Keeled 15
Dreaming the Dream Poetic 17
The Poetry in Life 18
Poison Arrow 20
Forsaken 21
And Here I Sit, the Life of the Party 22
On This Day, Deep, Somber and Gray 23
It's Okay to Be Afraid 24
You Can't Hold Me Back 25
Home Psychology 26
Suited in Traits and Actions 28
Fearing Wisely 29
For, I Too, Have Written Darkly 30
Cerulean Wings 32
Ice House Road 33
You and I Must Be 34
On Average, America 35
Light in the Darkness 39
Woman of My Dreams 40
Held Within the Sun 41
You Asked and I Answered 43
On the Wayside 44
Blood Sweat and Tears 45
A Cause Unknown 46
On Watch 47
Serenity 49
My Addiction 50
Love's Equation 51
Of All You Could Have Asked 52
Untangled, Unraveled 53

Sinner's Exile 55
Earn a Dollar to Spend a Dollar 57
The Wires of Life 59
A Walk in the Park (Shakespearean Sonnet) 61
Beyond the Pale 62
Unconnected Connection 63
Love's Duality 64
In This Life or Another 65
Easy-Going Woman 66
Ray of Hope 67
Prominence 68
Sun Rays 69
My Dear Friend 70
Stay on Top of Your Game (An Ode to Edward Segal Inc.) 71
In the Name of Love and Metaphor 73
We Americans Refacing the Nation 74
Pick Some Flowers 76
Till the End of Time 78
Glimpses 79
Something Clever, but Nothing Cliché 81
Straight from the Heart 82
Without You 83
The Rustle of the Leaves 84
Love's Taste 85
If There Is Ever 86
Love's Path 87
All That Is true, Lies in You 88
Cleansing 89
Cup of Joe 90
Without a Worry in the World 91
This One Goes out To... 92

BLACKOUT EDITION

A STEP INTO MY HEART

JOSEPH R. ADOMAVICIA

RP PUBLISHING

A POET IS A POEM UNWRITTEN

A poet is a poem

Joe Adomavicia,

is

written in codes;
and
complete novelties.

A poet is a poem

For me,
Joe Adomavicia,
strength and frailty
are the writer.
arteries
poetic blood,
diversity,

darkness
in the soul the poet.

A poet is a poem

For me,
Joe Adomavicia,
there is
a dream

a poet
and poems that are

home.

A STEP INTO MY HEART

in   my heart,

cross   e   d
and ravaged
battered
and bogged down.

in   my heart,
ta k   e
me,
across
waters streaming,

dirt paths
to a stone castle
without a master
but, be forewarned

of
eagle eyes atop his nest.

step into my heart,
talk with me
walk with me,
travel   winding halls

doors
jeweled in opal,

in   center chamber,
set your eyes
and decipher,

step into my heart
and see what it takes
to be me.

EVEN-KEELED

Even-keeled,
man's
voyage
of due time,
time passing.

captain of one,

captain of none.

seas un raveled –
glory revealed.

Even-keeled,

continues the voyage

rays of light to illuminate
integrity acquired.
prophets
of a man
standing tall.

For I am even-keeled

Captain of one,
and
captain of none.

DREAMING THE DREAM POETIC

Would it be wrong?

If only now I realized

a ll

the poetry in Life?

Would it be abstract?
To say I am,

poetry's poet
and did not know

that I am,
that me,
an ordinary Joe is
dreaming the dream poetic?

THE POETRY IN LIFE

Take two steps
Fix your eyes
Poetry

is life,
explicit beauty.

you hear it

you see it

you taste it

you smell it

letting in   bliss
that is the poetry in life.

POISON ARROW

a
piercing
blow

my
chest;

spilling
love's blood

mind, soul, and body
drained

now

I try my best

my hands
breaking,
trying to pull this
poison arrow from my chest.

FORSAKEN

try defining existence
so fragile.

Physically mentally

trapped in disdain.

running to the end

further away
trapped in this hell.

Why is it that I am forsaken?

AND HERE I SIT, THE LIFE OF THE PARTY

A
life
alone,
desolate,
barren,

people

lingering
And here I sit,
the life of the party

a face in the crowd

Somehow
too frail,
too shy,

I wait
I try

only to be knocked back down.

ON THIS DAY, DEEP, SOMBER AND GRAY

deep, gray,
all around me,

my skin

forming puddles on the concrete

and now

my being,
my senses,
paved in
gold.

IT'S OKAY TO BE AFRAID

It is okay

yesterday's fears
dissipate

It is okay to be afraid,

you are you
not them –

once more

It is okay to be afraid,

you are not alone.

YOU CAN'T HOLD ME BACK

Hit me,

my face,
my arms,
my legs,

Insult me,
it hurts,
your thirst,

can't hold me back.

my heart

my goals, my dreams,
what I

have
all

Satisfy

me

HOME PSYCHOLOGY

I am

the mountain

I am

just *a poem*

SUITED IN TRAITS AND ACTIONS

I

could

never

preach love
but not act
in the name of love

FEARING WISELY

I fear

this earth

FOR I, TOO, HAVE WRITTEN DARKLY

Write on,

you and I,

Each word,
each line,

We are one

the

reason

I

Write on,

We are one
you and I,

CERULEAN WINGS

stand   bold

Sing

songs of

thy heart

Cleansing,
within.

ICE HOUSE ROAD

beaten
trees lining the streets.
ana deep blues

paint the skies
my eyes.

even
down this winding road

of the old,

Where
an empty house, an empty soul,

and

truth
is as simple as

a white lie.

YOU AND I MUST BE

You must be

the
ebb and flow

I must be

the spring's
or gentle
azure bliss

You must be
the

cherry blossom's pink wave
of precious relation.

I must be
the
the vibrancy

of our existence,
love in orbit.

ON AVERAGE, AMERICA

live better lives.

lead America

govern collectively
work together

Wake up America.

show

our children,

so
they

live

everyday
the innocent
forecast.

Wake up America.

My intent
clear.

cowards   sit back,

Is that not   crazy?

reorganize

our acceptance

honor our freedom,

our

America,

a "United State",

LIGHT IN THE DARKNESS

in life

our heart
is

the

light in darkness

WOMAN OF MY DREAMS

My aim

My
woman

My
dreams,

I see her,

two hearts concur,

HELD WITHIN THE SUN

my dear
my love is yours

without fear.

my dear
my love is yours

held within the sun.

my dear
my love is yours

year round

to take your

hand,

to reassure you.

my love is yours for the taking.

YOU ASKED AND I ANSWERED

you
write for you,
I

am a vessel.
Poetry
flows through me,

ON THE WAYSIDE

sing songs courageously,
dreams are attainable,
leave fear
on the wayside.

shape
who you aim to be.

teach a lesson even
the most frightening trials
are a small nuisance

Leave the past behind,

Relish what you see
shape
who you aim to be.

BLOOD, SWEAT, AND TEARS

My brothers

through blood, sweat, and tears.

no doubt,

stand tall beside me,

As mentors,

grinding it out, milling and turning

Manufacturing
success,

shaping, honing, sharpening,
each others wits through,

A CAUSE UNKNOWN

I tell myself,

Life moves on,

wonder why

the blood
is shed,
for a cause unknown.

ON WATCH

Another shooting

a community

now
on watch

yell out

arise

try and help this city –

SERENITY

my

serenity

i s

held
in
the

H o r i z o N

MY ADDICTION

If I lost
you
at least

I'd be free of you.

LOVE'S EQUATION

To you,

love is

zilch, nothing, nada.

To me,

love

lead me to believe.

OF ALL YOU COULD HAVE ASKED

you
chose
to
disappoints

my heart

UNTANGLED, UNRAVELED

My heart,

untangled,
unraveled.

I don't hate you,

But,

cutting ties

and
carrying on
in these last words to you,

untangled,
unraveled.

SINNER'S EXILE

a Betrayal disclosed,

She

Who gifts such
evil deeds

your
gift of Deceit

my

deMeanor;

sorrow, regret, anguish and hurt,

Go,

without me.

Into sinner's exile.

EARN A DOLLAR TO SPEND A DOLLAR

a dollar

makes the world go 'round.

We all know
by now,

upper class or poor,

does it even
matter anymore?

a dollar

makes the world go 'round.

selling the meaning of life

to survive.

Earn a dollar
to spend a dollar,

make the world go 'round.

THE WIRES OF LIFE

The wires of life have frayed.

Revert
to a time

when

the modern mind

was not so
juxtaposed.

A time when

people

w e re

not afraid

A WALK IN THE PARK (SHAKESPEAREAN SONNET)

Autumn's bright blue sky,

winds and
gentle hymns

Find your way back to me

BEYOND THE PALE

my life's on repeat,

at my table, hear told a tale of

undistinguished anguished pieces of stone screams,

glance upon my face, my mind,

beyond the pale.

UNCONNECTED CONNECTION

she is my

star upon the sky
and

she is there,
smiling, in her
extravagance,

connected
Somehow, someway,
in my reality,

LOVE'S DUALITY

Your love is like

Cobain's cocaine;

Marilyn's heroin;

Marley's Mary Jane;

Jimi's yellow sunshine;

and keeps me coming back for more.

IN THIS LIFE OR ANOTHER

If we see each other again,

I pray   you don't walk by,

whether it be in this life or another,

make effort to climb any mountain for me,
I will be there   awaiting your grace

praying to hear of your success.

EASY-GOING WOMAN

easy-going woman
rock my world

send me into a swirl –

decipher my mind's hieroglyph –

and we could run true,

how I need you,
oh, yes I do –

rock my world and

translate   dreams into reality.

RAY OF HOPE

I have survived –

the sun rises,
and I am me
undoubtedly.

PROMINENCE

you,

your eyes.

I see the truest –
the divine.

you,
your touch
is able to mend
my consciousness.

you,
your nature,
has will enough to enrapture
m e

you,

ar e
the prominence in my world.

SUN RAYS

Two little bundles of joy –
Dylan,
Ariya,

Your Uncle Joe Joe loves you so so much.

you a re.
My happiness

my glorious sun rays,

MY DEAR FRIEND

I haven't been the same since that day.

Taken
without
all the days that could have come.

How I would love to see you.

Wishing I could regress

To say "I love you and I'll miss you."
My dear friend, Dwight Nadeau.

STAY ON TOP OF YOUR GAME (AN ODE TO EDWARD SEGAL INC.)

I'm tellin' ya',
stay on top of your game.

Never admit defeat,
beat
all of that doubt
good and dead.

If not,
you'll find
shame
disgust
and lust
for the aplomb of those
who trust
in themselves.

I'm tellin' ya',
stay on top of your game.

If not,
who knows
where
the currents will pull you.

IN THE NAME OF LOVE AND METAPHOR

I bring a rose say I love you,
unconditionally
100 times over again –

to

hear the sounds of our hearts pumping in unison
and feel your taste as I inhaled your embrace,
savoring
the fact that we as the flower and the petals
of what was and will be,

fulfilling destiny
in the name of love and metaphor.

WE AMERICANS REFACING THE NATION

our country
one big puzzle.

Artfully pretending
we are
one poem,
same puzzle.

The different pieces,
individual unique shaped.

  let us
segregate ourselves,
in Unity,

we, Americans,
one nation that never ceases to
reface for the better.

PICK SOME FLOWERS

and drop them by my grave.
Read my poems and pass them on –

another day
is not too far away.

Smile
and remember me

and when our hearts felt glory.
Play as we played,
work as we worked,

And
inherit me.

my friends –
my family.

Pick some flowers

Read my poems and

carry   on your way,
another day

to live eternally

TILL THE END OF TIME

from now

till the end of time,

the truth

of the matter is

the mere thought of you,
of us, must die.

GLIMPSES

by the river,

fishing

riding our bikes,
up and down the hills,
working a sweat going up
and when we soared down
the wind,
it felt liberating.

I catch myself thinking of you

here and there

about memories we shared,
and when every one of them started,
everyone   ended,

my dear departed.

SOMETHING CLEVER BUT, NOTHING CLICHÉ

I have been thinking

if I sang a line,
even two, you would

smile brighter
than sunshine on the ocean.

I have been thinking of u
s

two star struck lovers,

under a star kissed sky,

and would take your hand,
because there is no other
in heart or mind.

STRAIGHT FROM THE HEART

I knew it from the start
that you were my type of woman.

we click on several levels.

Straight from the heart,

I knew it from the start

I

want you,
in the winter, spring, summer and fall.

The man to
feel passion that only comes
straight from the heart.

WITHOUT YOU

what would I do

if I were to lose you?

death is eventual,
my love perpetual.

what would I do

if I were to lose you?
I'd live for you,
the least I could do.

THE RUSTLE OF THE LEAVES

I spoke softly

to the winds of old
as
the rustle of the leaves.

    left me a wayward soul,
yet,

    one day,
my wings will spread

within the trace
of your guidance.

LOVE'S TASTE

The beauty of getting to know someone,

is accepting
and

is cherishing all of
love's taste in a new flavor.

IF THERE IS EVER

If there is

ever a

moment,
your heart feels broken,

and

soul feels lost,
please, don't worry;

soul mate there
will always be a piece of you
inside of me.

LOVE'S PATH

I understand

            life moves on.
Beyond my
                                    life
and
I understand love's path
        spins the thread of life,

and   the Inevitable,
severs with abhorred shears.

ALL THAT IS TRUE, LIES IN YOU

I'm not sure

what it is yet,

and I can't quite

put my finger on it,
but, it is

as if all that was ever true, lies in you.

CLEANSING

No longer afraid

I begin to cleanse my life

of
the fakes, the snakes,

drenched in deceit;

No longer afraid

here I come,

face to face
with the harbinger of hate,

in honor of my dignity.

A CUP OF JOE

I'm not the Joe

you know ?

I'm living free

A priceless portrait

never to be forgotten,

my heart
my life

Articulate a
foundation laid level.

I'm not the Joe
You used to know,

Wind at my back, living to grow.

WITHOUT A WORRY IN THE WORLD

I have come to a point in my life,

where I smile freely,

where love permeates

where forgiveness trumps grudges,

where success is the only option,
my dreams are within my grasp;

without a worry in the world.

THIS ONE GOES OUT TO . . .

all the harlots
the starlets,
the piece of my heart
left it in the past.

You taught me
to let the dust settle before I rage.

This one goes out to all of the demons

I am a new man, with a new plan, my life, in my hands.

You taught me

my artistry defines me,
it is my shield
against a critic ephemeral.